Progressi
BLUES
ACOUSTIC
GUITAR
METHOD

by

Brett Duncan

MW01131032

Visit our Website
www.learntoplaymusic.com

Koala Publications

The Progressive Series of Music Instruction Books, CDs, Videos and DVDs

CONTENTS

INTRODUCTION

Progressive Blues Acoustic Guitar Method covers all the important aspects of Acoustic Blues Guitar. This book introduces popular Blues progressions, Blues Rhythms, Basic Blues Lead Guitar Patterns and Lead Guitar Techniques. You will learn how to combine Blues rhythms and Blues licks, fingerpicking Blues styles such as the Constant Bass Line style and the Alternating Thumb style and an introduction to Acoustic Slide guitar. It will be helpful to already have a basic knowledge of guitar before you tackle the examples in this book. *Progressive Guitar Method Book 1: Beginner* and *Progressive Guitar Method: Rhythm* are recommended as introductory manuals to this book.

Blues rhythm patterns are explained clearly and simply throughout the book, with the help of an *Easy Read* system involving arrows. Blues lead guitar licks are explained with the use of tablature, an easy read system for reading notes.

All the basic ingredients of Blues acoustic guitar playing are introduced over the course of this book. All examples are recorded on the accompanying CD and are fun to play as well as being authentic and informative. Anyone who completes this book will have a good grasp of the basics of Blues acoustic guitar playing and will be able to make some great sounds in a fairly short time.

For more information on the *Progressive* guitar series contact;
Koala Publications
email: info@koalapublications.com
or visit our website;
www.learntoplaymusic.com

COPYRIGHT CONDITIONS
No part of this book can be reproduced in any form without the written consent of the publishers.
© 1997 Nermyco Pty Ltd

Special thanks to Thom Burns for use of his instrument.

Using the Compact Disc

It is recommended that you have a copy of the accompanying compact disc that includes all the examples in this book. The book shows you where to put your fingers and what technique to use and the recording lets you hear how each example should sound. Practice the examples slowly at first, gradually increasing tempo. Once you are confident you can play the example evenly without stopping the beat, try playing along with the recording. You will hear a drum beat at the beginning of each example, to lead you into the example and to help you keep time. To play along with the CD your guitar must be in tune with it. If you have tuned using an electronic tuner (see below) your guitar will already be in tune with the CD. A small diagram of a compact disc with a number as shown below indicates a recorded example. If you do not know how to tune your guitar see *Progressive Guitar Method Book 1: Beginner.*

12 ← **Track Number**

Electronic Tuner

The easiest and most accurate way to tune your guitar is by using an **electronic tuner.** An electronic tuner allows you to tune each string individually to the tuner, by indicating whether the notes are sharp (too high), or flat (too low). If you have an electric guitar you can plug it directly in to the tuner. If you have an acoustic guitar the tuner will have an inbuilt microphone. There are several types of electronic guitar tuners but

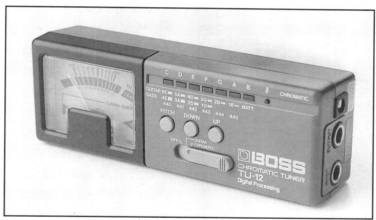

Electronic Tuner

most are relatively inexpensive and simple to operate. Tuning using other methods is difficult for beginning guitarists and it takes many months to master. So we recommend you purchase an electronic tuner, particularly if you do not have a guitar teacher or a friend who can tune it for you. Also if your guitar is way out of tune you can always take it to your local music store so they can tune it for you. Once a guitar has been tuned correctly it should only need minor adjustments before each practice session.

Tuning Your Guitar to the CD

Before you commence each lesson or practice session you will need to tune your guitar. If your guitar is out of tune everything you play will sound incorrect even though you are holding the correct notes. On the accompanying CD the **first six tracks** correspond to the **six strings of the guitar**.

 1 **6th String**
E Note (Thickest string)

 2 **5th String**
A Note

 3 **4th String**
D Note

 4 **3rd String**
G Note

 5 **2nd String**
B Note

 6 **1st String**
E Note (Thinnest string)

CHORD DIAGRAMS USED IN THIS BOOK

Chords are learnt with the help of a **chord diagram**. This will show you exactly where to place your left hand fingers in order to play a particular chord. A chord diagram is a grid of horizontal and vertical lines representing the strings and frets of the guitar as shown below.

LEFT HAND FINGERING

❶ Index Finger
❷ Middle Finger
❸ Ring Finger
❹ Little Finger

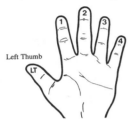

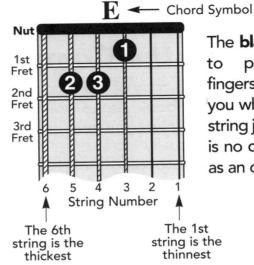

The **black dots** show you where to place your left hand fingers. The **white number** tells you which finger to place on the string just before the fret. If there is no dot on a string, you play it as an open (not fretted) string.

The other chord diagram symbols used in this book are summarised with the following two chord shapes.

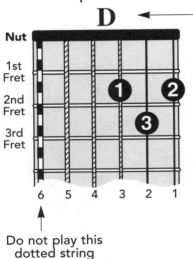

Chord symbol for **D major** chord.

A **dotted** string indicates that string is not to be strummed. An **X** on the string indicates that string is to **dampened** by another finger lightly touching it. The string is still strummed as a part of the chord but it is not heard.

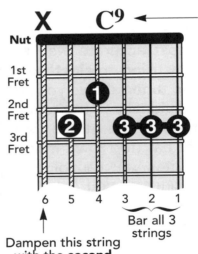

Chord symbol for **C ninth** chord.

A small **bar** connecting several black dots indicates they are held down by the same finger. This is called **barring.**

❷ = Key Note

SCALE DIAGRAMS USED IN THIS BOOK

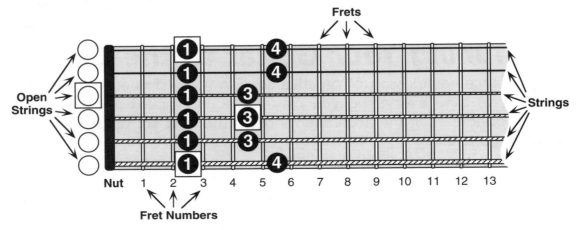

● or ○ = A note used in the scale or pattern.

■● or □○ = Indicates the note is the root note of the scale.

❷ = The number refers to the left hand fingering.

TABLATURE

Tablature is a method of indicating the position of notes on the fretboard. There are six "tab" lines each representing one of the six strings on the guitar.

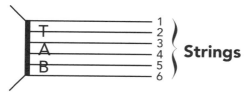

When a number is placed on one of the lines, it indicates the fret location of the note e.g.

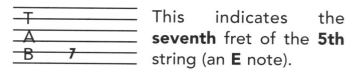 This indicates the **seventh** fret of the **5th** string (an **E** note).

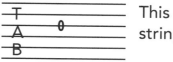 This indicates the **3rd** string open (a **G** note).

TABLATURE SYMBOLS

The following tablature symbols will appear throughout this book.

Hammer-On
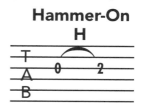

Pull-Off
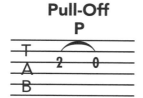

Slide
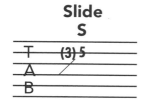

Bend
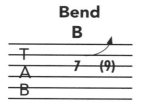

Release Bend
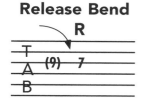

Vibrato

Trill
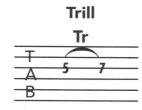

RHYTHM SYMBOLS

The following rhythm symbols will appear throughout this book.

V **Down-strum**
Strum all strings within chord, using a downward motion.

∧ **Up-strum**
Strum the first 2-3 strings using an upward motion.

V **Miss**
Miss the strings on a downward motion.

V **Short Down-strum**
Strum only 2-3 strings of chord, using a downward motion.

D **Right Hand Damp**
 Mute strings with right hand while strumming.

LESSON ONE

BLUES PROGRESSIONS

Before working your way through this book it will be important to have a basic understanding of a **Blues chord progression**. Most Blues songs follow a common sequence of chords with each chord played for a certain amount of bars.

A Blues progression is generally constructed from the three basic chords in a key which are illustrated in the table below. These three chords are referred to as the **I, IV** and **V** chords. The Roman numerals relating to the **1st, 4th,** and **5th** notes of the major scale from which each chord takes its name.

Key →	A	A#/B♭	B	C	C#/D♭	D	D#/E♭	E	F	F#/G♭	G	G#/A♭
I	A	A#/B♭	B	C	C#/D♭	D	D#/E♭	E	F	F#/G♭	G	G#/A♭
IV	D	D#/E♭	E	F	F#/G♭	G	G#/A♭	A	A#/B♭	B	C	C#/D♭
V	E	F	F#/G♭	G	G#/A♭	A	A#/B♭	B	C	C#/D♭	D	D#/E♭

TWELVE BAR BLUES PROGRESSION

The **twelve bar Blues progression** is the most common chord sequence used in Blues. There are many variations of this progression. The example below consists of four bars of the **I** chord, two bars of the **IV** chord, two bars of the **I** chord, one of the **V** chord, one bar of the **IV** chord and two bars of the **I** chord.

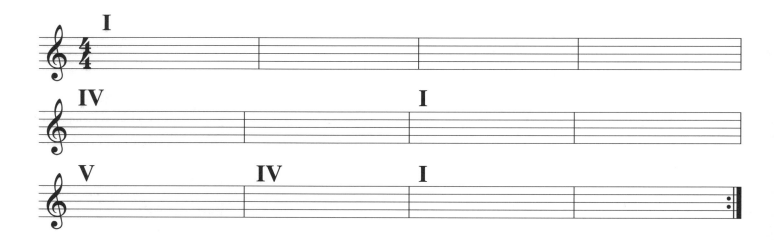

To play the previous progression in the **key of A**, substitute the symbols **I**, **IV**, and **V** with the three basic chords in the **key of A** (**A**, **D** and **E**), as shown in the table on the previous page.

To play the first example, use basic chords and use the suggested rhythm pattern. After playing the 12 bars, finish with one strum of the first chord (**A**).

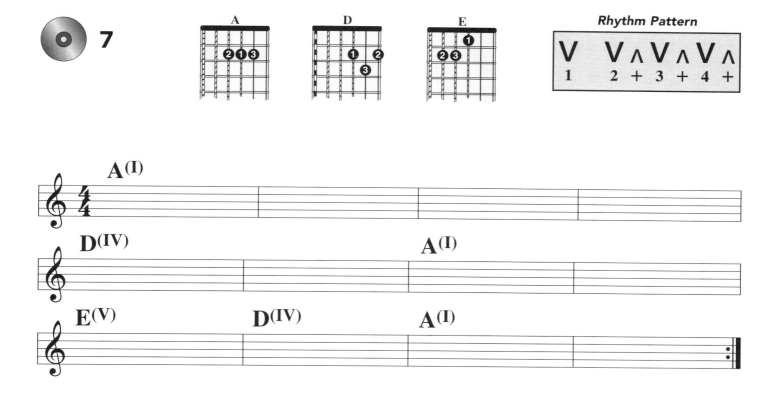

To play the same progression in the **key of C**, substitute the symbols **I**, **IV** and **V** with the three basic chords in the **key of C** (**C**, **F** and **G**), as shown in the table on the previous page.

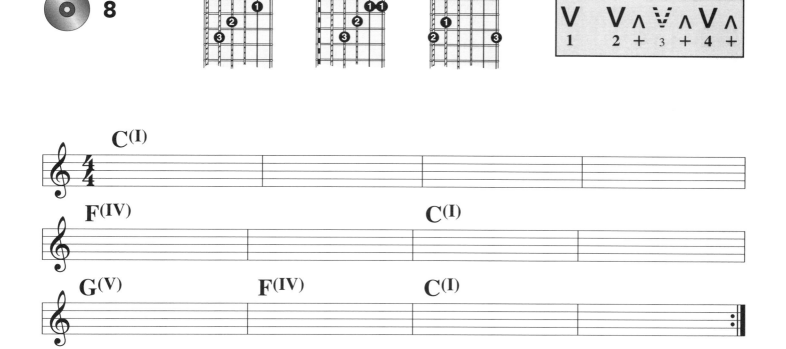

VARIATIONS ON THE TWELVE BAR BLUES PROGRESSION

As mentioned previously there are many variations of the 12 bar Blues progression. The first of these variations inserts the **V** chord in the **12th** bar. Try the following example in the **key of A**.

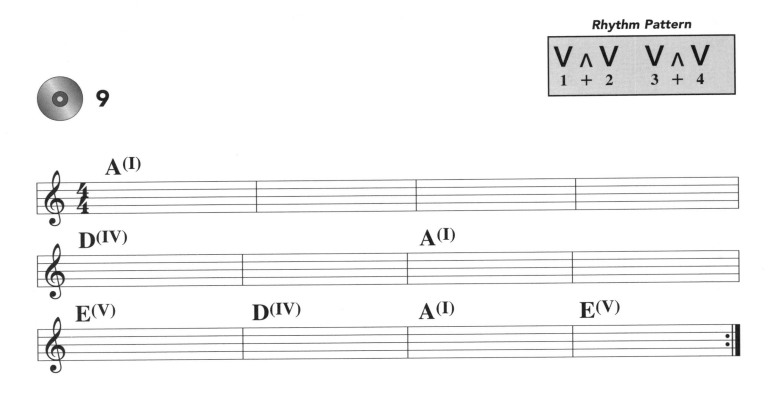

Another variation is to insert the **IV** chord in bar 2 before returning to the **I** chord in bar 3. Example 10 is in the **key of C**. Don't forget to finish with one strum of the first chord (**C**).

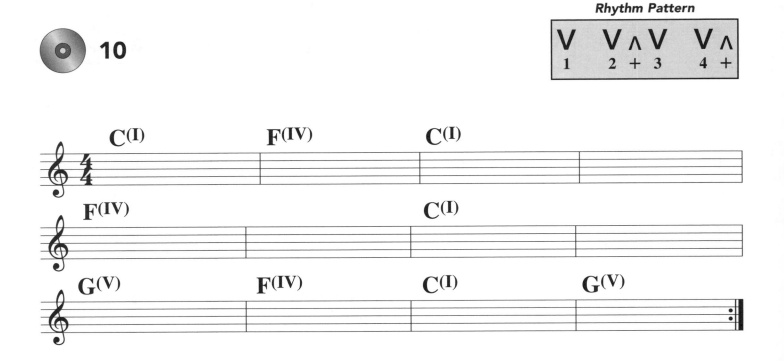

Another common variation on the 12 bar Blues progression is to substitute the major chord with a **seventh** chord. This definitely helps provide a more "bluesy" sound to the progression. The following example makes use of the seventh chord. This time the key chosen is **E**.

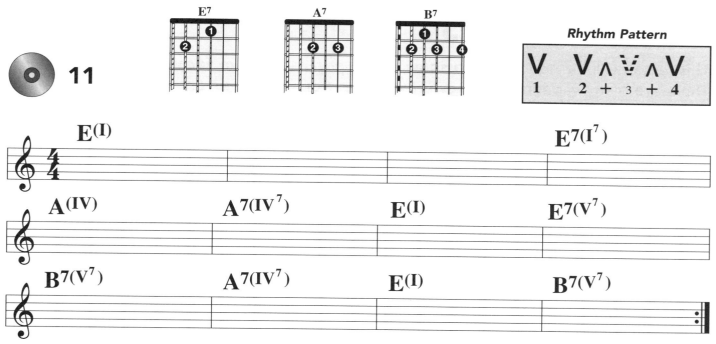

EIGHT BAR BLUES PROGRESSION

Another common Blues progression is the **eight bar Blues progression**. A variation of this sequence is shown below, two bars of the **I** chord, two bars of the **IV** chord, one bar of the **I** chord, one bar of the **V** chord and two bars of the **I** chord.

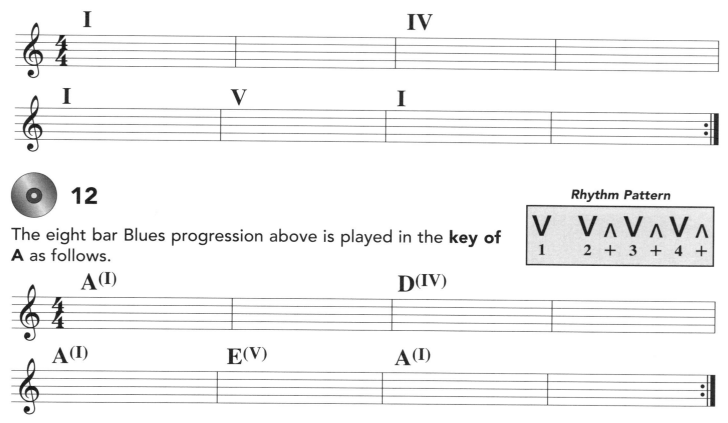

The eight bar Blues progression above is played in the **key of A** as follows.

As with the 12 bar Blues progression there are several variations on the 8 bar blues progression, some of which will appear throughout the book.

LESSON TWO

BLUES RHYTHMS

This lesson will introduce you to some of the popular **rhythm techniques** used in Blues. There are many variations on these rhythms but only the basic and most common Blues rhythms will be discussed.

TRIPLET RHYTHMS

A **triplet rhythm** is created by strumming three evenly spaced strums per beat (a total of twelve strums per bar). The first of each three strums must be played slightly stronger or louder than the other two strums within a beat. This is best achieved by using a long strum (striking all the strings of a chord) on each beat of the bar, and using a short strum (middle two or three strings only) on the other strums. This is represented below using big and small strumming symbols. The rhythm is counted **1 and ah 2 and ah 3 and ah 4 and ah**, written as **1 + a, 2 + a, 3 + a, 4 + a**.

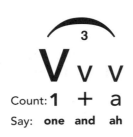

  13

Play the following rhythm pattern holding an **E7** chord.

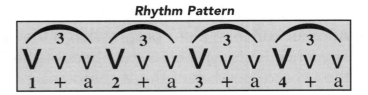

Apply the triplet rhythm to the following 12 Bar Blues progression in **E**.

 **14**

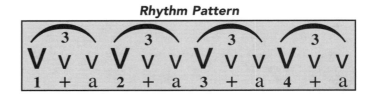

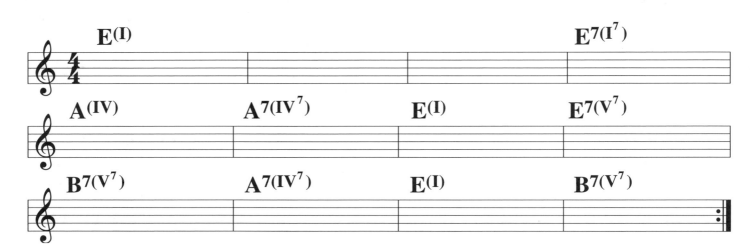

It will be essential to be familiar with some triplet rhythm variations. The following example uses a rhythm counted as **1, 2 and ah, 3 and ah, 4.** This time the **key of G** is used.

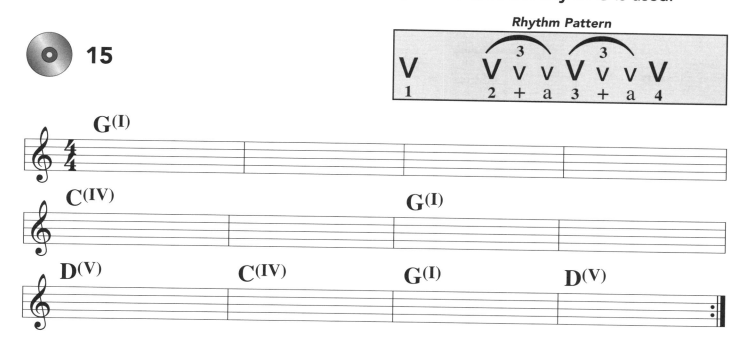

The next example is another triplet variation over an 8 bar Blues progression.

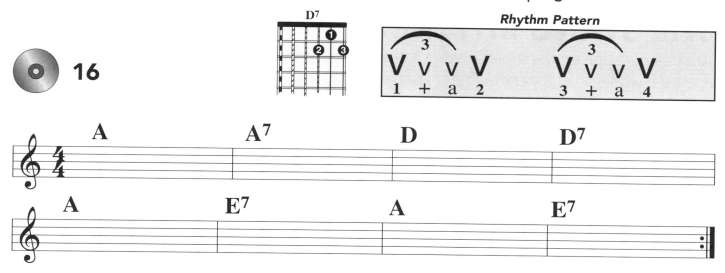

Example 17 features chord changes every 2 beats (a total of six strums to a chord).

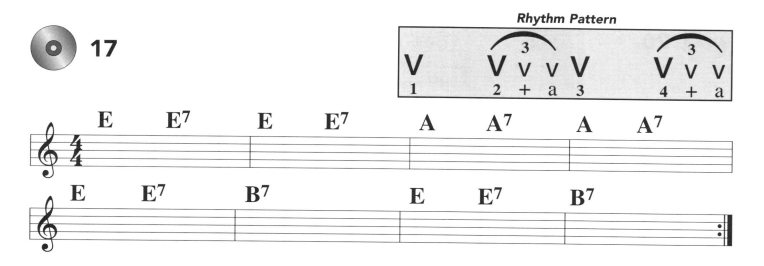

It is also common to miss the middle strum within a triplet group. The next example uses a rhythm counted as "**1 ... ah, 2 ... ah, 3 ... ah, 4 ... ah**".

Bars 11 and 12 introduces a popular ending to a 12 bar Blues progression.

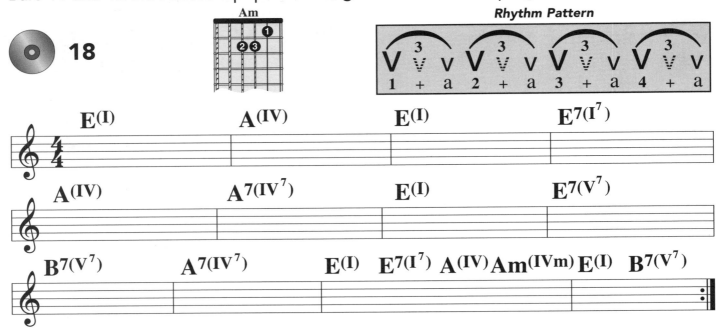

THE SWING RHYTHM

Another variation on the triplet rhythm is the **swing rhythm**, produced by slightly delaying the up-strum within an eighth note rhythm pattern. The rhythm is counted the same as the rhythm in the previous example except an up-strum is used on the count "**a**". This rhythm is often used on a song with a faster tempo. Listen to the recording to get the feel for this rhythm.

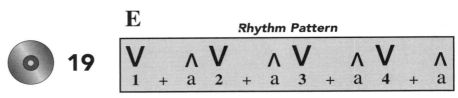

The **major sixth** chord is featured in the following example.

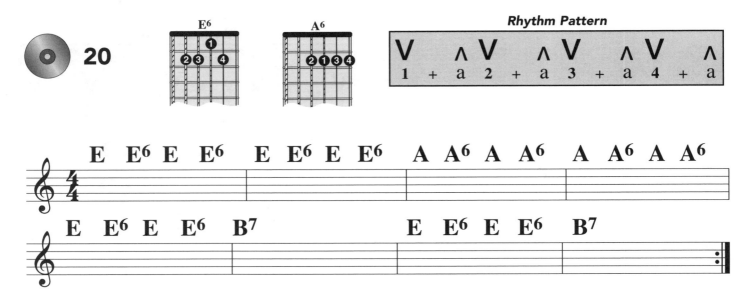

LESSON THREE

THE SHUFFLE RHYTHM

The **shuffle rhythm** "boogie" is another popular rhythm used in Blues. Two types of chords are used to play the shuffle rhythm, the two string form of the major chord and the two string form of the sixth chord. These chords are easiest played in the open position. Shown below are the **A, D, E, A6, D6** and **E6** chords. The sixth chords are played with the **third** finger but the **first** finger should remain positioned on the **fifth** chord as indicated by the open circle.

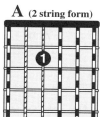 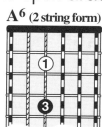 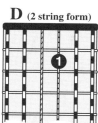 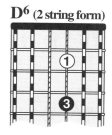 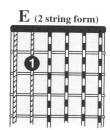 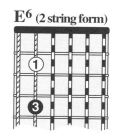

 21

Example 21 uses the **A** and **A6** chords. The rhythm is counted as "**1...ah, 2...ah, 3...ah, 4...ah**". Listen to the recording to get the right feel for this rhythm.

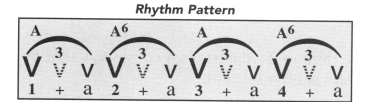

RIGHT HAND DAMPING

A popular effect to use with the shuffle rhythm is **right hand damping** (indicated by the symbol **D**). This is achieved by lightly resting the butt of the right hand on the strings near the bridge of the guitar while strumming, producing a slightly muted sound to the chord. Do not press too heavily on the strings as the chord will be completely muted creating a "dead" sound instead. This technique is applied to the following example.

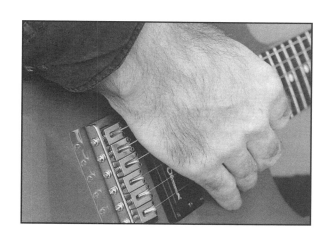

The next example features the above chords over an 8 bar Blues progression.

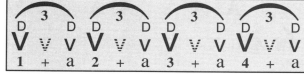

 22

The shuffle rhythm is often applied to a 12 bar Blues progression.

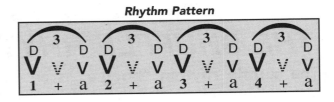

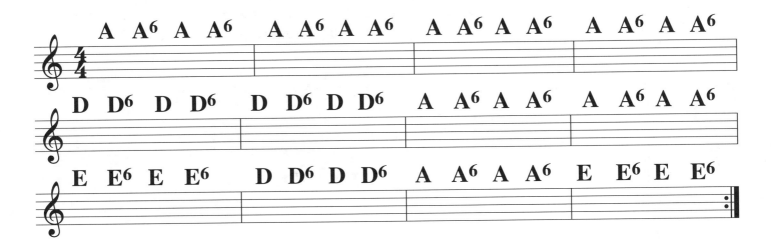

Example 24 illustrates a common variation of the shuffle rhythm.

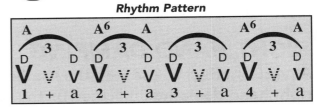

The chord sequence from the previous example can be applied to a 12 bar Blues progression in the **key of A**.

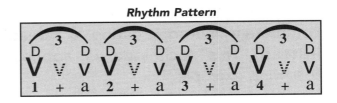

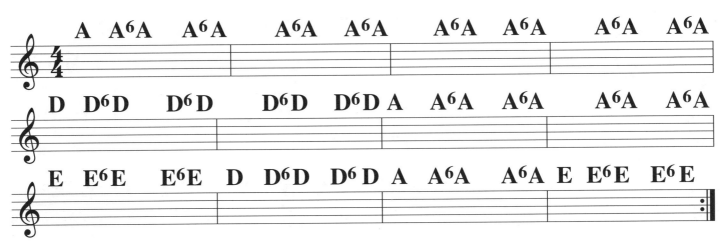

Another popular chord shape applied to a shuffle rhythm is the 2 string form of the **seventh** chord. Study the following diagrams.

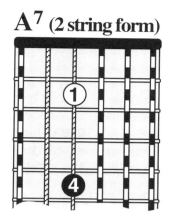
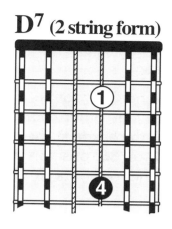
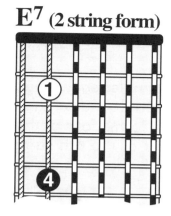

The 2 string form of the seventh chord is often used in conjunction with the shuffle rhythm.

 26

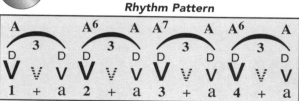

The next example is a popular variation of the previous rhythm.

 27

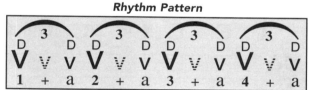

The following 12 bar Blues progression utilises the chord sequence of the previous example to the other chords in the **key of A**.

 28

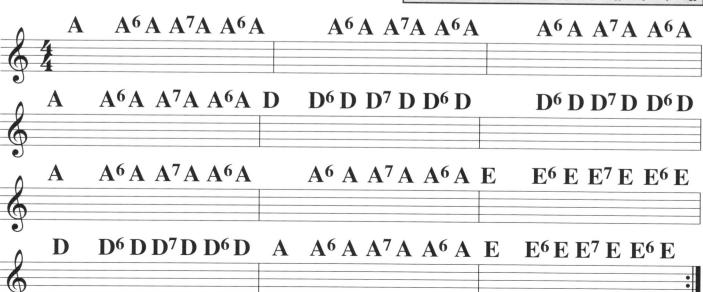

SHUFFLE RHYTHM (CLOSED POSITION)

To use the shuffle rhythm with chords other than the chords used in the previous examples, the following chord shapes are used. These shapes may be played in either the root six or root five position, i.e. the root note or the name of the chord is found on either the **6th** or **5th** string.

The examples shown below are the **G** and **G6** (root note on the **6th** string), and the **C** and **C6** (root note found on the **5th** string). To play other chords, for example **F** or **F6**, position the root six formations of the major and sixth chords at the **first** fret as the root note (**F**) is on the **first** fret of the **6th** string. To play a **B** or **B6**, position the root five formations of the major and sixth chords at the **second** fret as the root note (**B**) is on the **second** fret of the **5th** string.

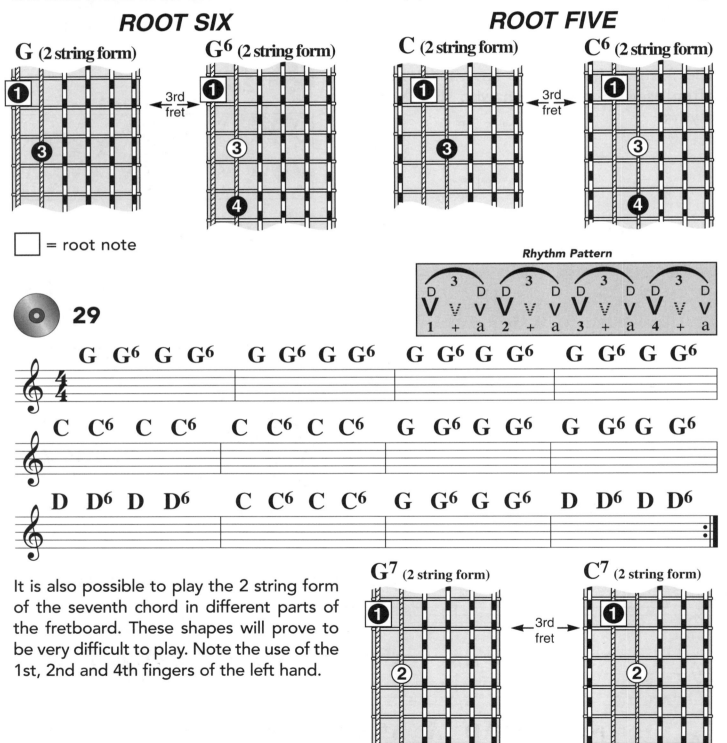

It is also possible to play the 2 string form of the seventh chord in different parts of the fretboard. These shapes will prove to be very difficult to play. Note the use of the 1st, 2nd and 4th fingers of the left hand.

LESSON FOUR

BASIC BLUES LEAD GUITAR

This lesson will introduce you to the basics of **Blues lead guitar**. The examples in this lesson are played only within the first position (first 4 or 5 frets of the guitar). Lead guitar is played with the help of a lead guitar pattern. The pattern refers to the location of the notes on the fretboard of a particular scale. The two most common patterns (or scales) are shown below in the open position, the minor pentatonic scale and the Blues scale.

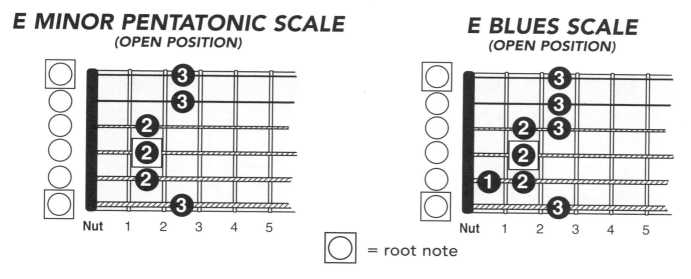

E MINOR PENTATONIC SCALE
(OPEN POSITION)

E BLUES SCALE
(OPEN POSITION)

⬜ = root note

Practice the following examples which ascend and descend the **E minor** pentatonic scale and **E** Blues scale until you are familiar with them.

30.0

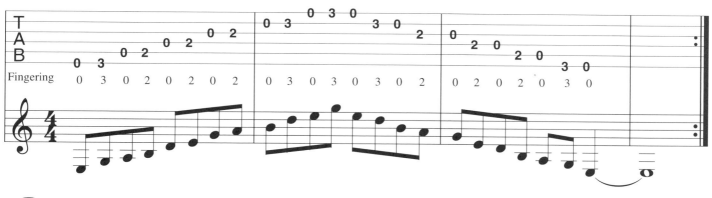

30.1

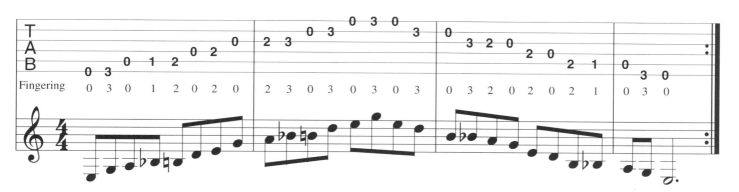

The **E minor** pentatonic and the **E Blues** scales can be used to play a lick or solo over a chord progression in the **key of E**. Try the following examples and notice that each note played is taken directly from the **E minor** pentatonic or **E Blues** scale.

COMBINING SHUFFLE AND LEAD

It is common practise to combine the shuffle with a lick in the open position. Try the following exercise which alternates between a basic E chord shuffle and a lick taken directly from the previous example. The symbol *N.C.* means no chord is played.

33

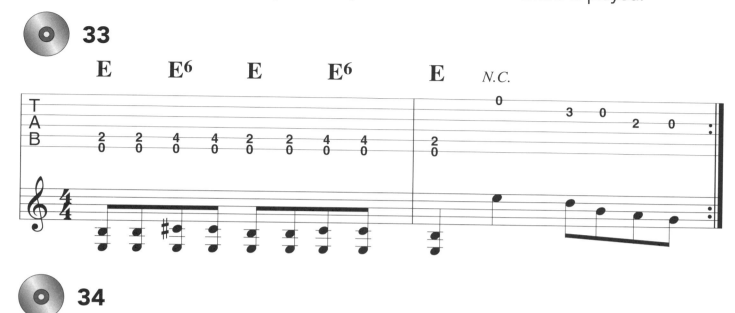

34

Now try applying the principal from the previous example to an entire 12 Bar Blues progression.

The next example incorporates the seventh chord.

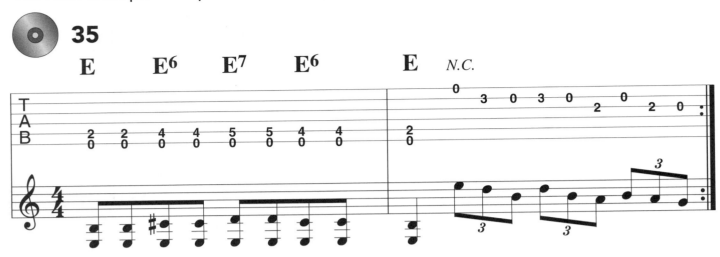

Now apply the previous combination of shuffle and lead to a 12 bar Blues progression.

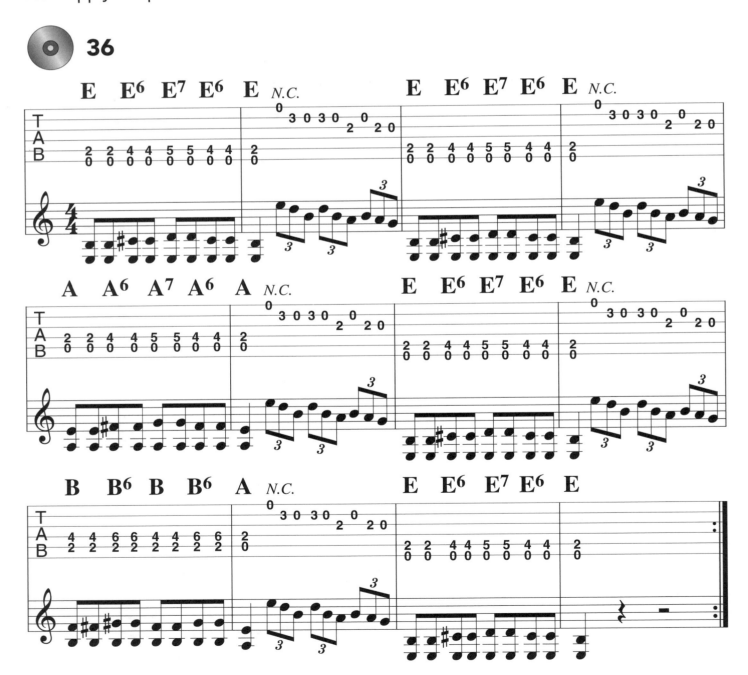

LESSON FIVE

OPEN POSITION SCALES IN THE KEY OF A

Another popular key to use in the open position is the key of A. Study the following diagrams.

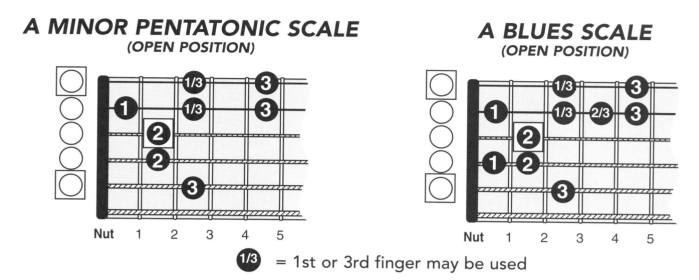

A MINOR PENTATONIC SCALE
(OPEN POSITION)

A BLUES SCALE
(OPEN POSITION)

1/3 = 1st or 3rd finger may be used

Practice the following examples which ascend and descend the **A minor** pentatonic scale and **A** Blues scale until you are familiar with them.

 37

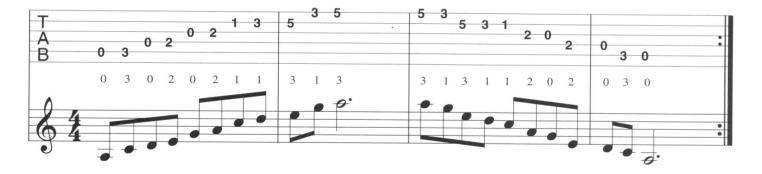

 **38**

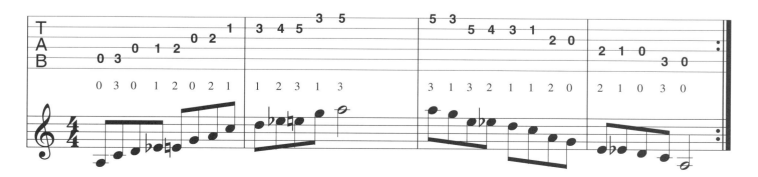

The following examples are played within the key of A.

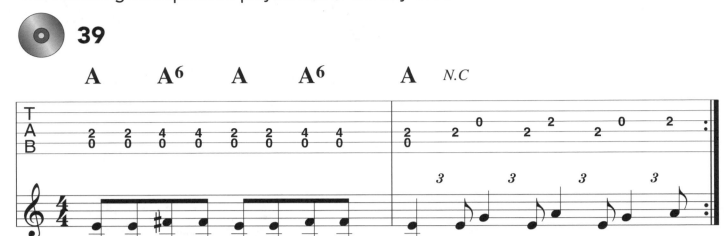

The next example uses the above lick throughout a 12 bar Blues progression in A.

Now apply the previous combination of shuffle and lead to a 12 bar Blues progression. A variety of licks are used in this example.

LESSON SIX

BLUES LEAD GUITAR TECHNIQUES

This lesson will introduce several popular Blues lead guitar techniques which can be applied to any open position Blues lick.

THE HAMMER-ON

The **Hammer-on** is the first of several techniques you will learn as you work in this lesson. The hammer-on is a left hand technique which may be incorporated into a lick or solo. The hammer-on produces a note artificially by hammering a finger of the left hand onto a string. The impact of the string against the fretboard will cause the string to sound the note of the hammered fret. This technique is demonstrated below.

In order to play example 43, first play the open **third**. As the note is sounding, hammer the **second** finger of the **left** hand onto the **second** fret of the same string. If played correctly the note of the **second** fret will be produced. The hammer-on is indicated by a curved line and the symbol "**H**".

43

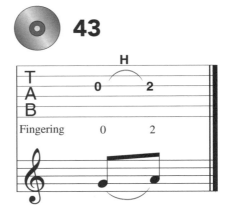

Begin by playing the open **third** string.

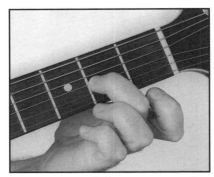

Hammer **second** finger onto the **second** fret of the **3rd** string.

Using the hammer-on will help create a much smoother flowing lick. This is shown below in the following examples. Examples 44 and 45 are the same lick except a hammer-on is used in example 45.

44

45

THE PULL-OFF

The **pull-off** is another popular left hand technique which can be applied to a lead guitar lick or lead guitar solo. The pull-off produces a note artificially with the left hand. This time a left hand finger is pulled away from the the string after fretting the note. If played correctly, the action of the finger leaving the string will cause the string to sound. This technique is demonstrated in Example 46. In order to play Example 46, play the **second** fret of the **3rd** string with the **second** finger of the **left** hand. Pull the **second** finger away from the string, with a slight plucking motion. If played correctly the note of the open string will be produced. The pull-off is indicated by a curved line and the symbol "**P**".

 46

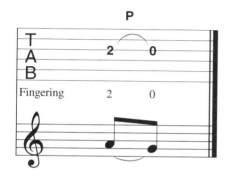

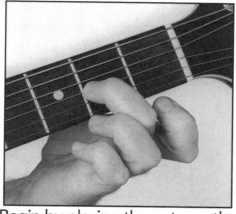

Begin by playing the note on the **second** fret of the **3rd** string.

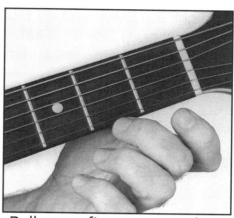

Pull away finger to produce note of the open string.

The pull-off can be used in a lick where a lower note follows a higher note on the same string. Using the pull-off will also help create a much smoother flowing lick. This is shown below in the following examples. Examples 47 and 48 are the same lick except a pull-off is used in example 48.

 47

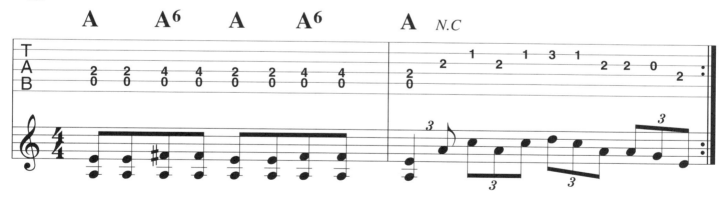

 48

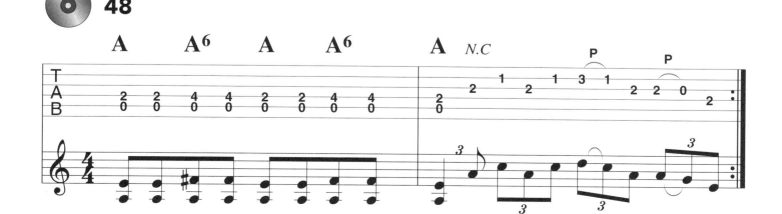

THE SLIDE

The **slide** is another popular left hand technique which can be applied to a lead guitar lick or lead guitar solo. This technique involves sliding between two notes on the same string whilst still fretting the string firmly against the fretboard. If played correctly the sound of the second note is produced artificially. The second note is not played with the right hand. This lesson outlines the different types of slides which can be used.

The letter "**S**" and a **straight line** indicates a slide. If the line comes from **below** the number, slide from a **lower** fret. If the line comes from **above** the number, slide form a **higher** fret. The number in the brackets is the suggested fret from which to slide from. In this situation the first of the two notes should contain no time value. In the following example a third type of slide is given. A straight line between two tab numbers indicates the first note should be held for a time value before sliding. Listen to the recording to hear the effect of this technique. The accompanying photos illustrate the first and most common type of slides, sliding from a lower fret to a higher fret.

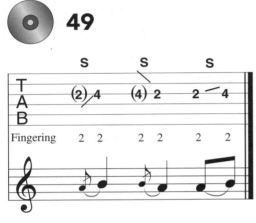

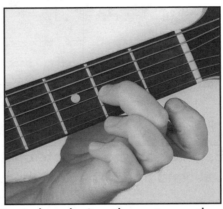

Begin by playing the note on the **second** fret of the **3rd** string.

Slide to **fourth** fret, still pressing firmly against fretboard.

The slide can be used anywhere within lead guitar pattern one between two notes on the same string. Examples 50 and 51 are the same lick except slides are used in example 51.

THE TRILL

The next technique to learn is the "Trill", indicated in the tab by the symbol **Tr**. Trills can add drama to your playing as well as being an important way of sustaining a note. A Trill is a rapid succession of hammer-ons and pull-offs with only the first note being picked. Listen to the recording to hear the correct effect of this technique.

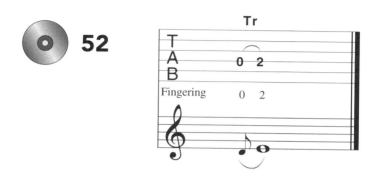

First try example 53, a simple lick in the **key of E**.

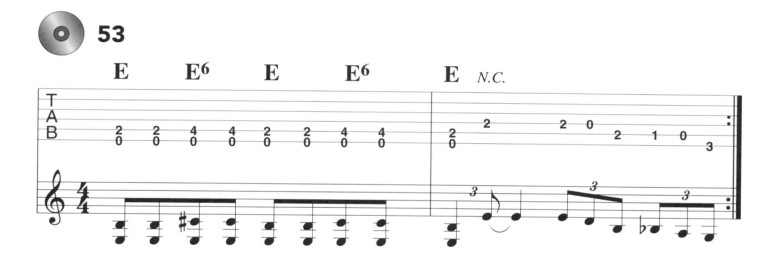

Now try example 54, the same lick as example 53 but the Trill is added.

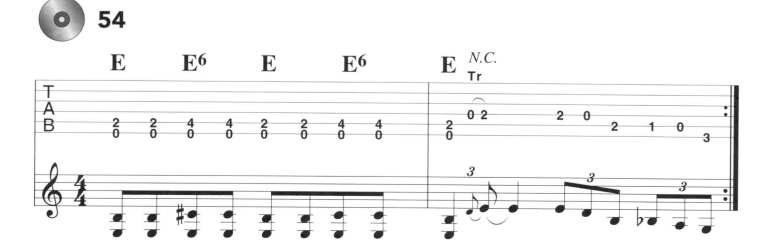

TURNAROUND LICK NO. 1 IN E
A turnaround lick is a familiar Blues lick played at the end of a Blues progression.

 55

 56

The next example utilises all the techniques discussed in this lesson including the above turnaround lick.

LESSON SEVEN

ADVANCED LEAD GUITAR TECHNIQUES

In this lesson you will be introduced to four commonly used Blues lead guitar techniques; the bend, the release bend, the double-note lick and vibrato. These techniques will prove to be more difficult than the previous techniques discussed and will require a great deal more practice to develop.

THE BEND

The **bend** is achieved by **bending** a string with the **left** hand in the direction of the **adjacent** strings, causing the note to rise in pitch. This is done with the **left** hand finger which is fretting the note. This technique is demonstrated in the following example. In Example 57, the note on the **third** fret of the **2nd** string is bent with the **third** finger of the **left** hand. In order to bend the note successfully, bend the string with the help of the **second** finger as well. This can be seen in the accompanying photograph. The symbol "**B**" and a curved line indicate a bend.

57

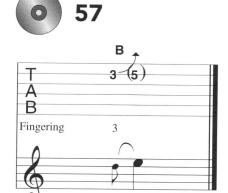

Play the note on the **third** fret of the **2nd** string.

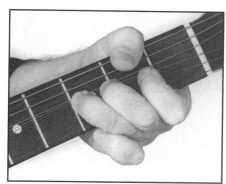

The **third** finger bends the string upwards, with the help of the **second** finger.

58 First try Example 58, a simple lick played in the **key of E**.

59 Now try Example 59, a similar lick to Example 58, but bends are added.

THE RELEASE BEND

The **release bend** is played by first **bending** the note indicated with the **left** hand, **plucking** the string whilst bent, then returning the string to its normal position. If played correctly the release bend creates a drop in pitch from a **higher** note to a **lower** note.

In order to play Example 60, bend the note on the **3rd** string, **second** fret with the **second** finger of the **left** hand. Pluck the **3rd** string with the **right** hand while the string is bent. Immediately after striking the string and still maintaining pressure on the note against the fretboard release the string carefully to its normal position. The release bend is indicated by a curved line and the symbol "**R**".

60

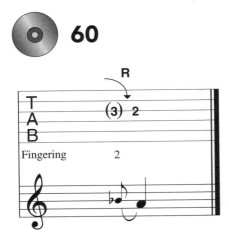

Bend the note on the **second** fret of the **3rd** string.

After the note is played, release the string to its normal position.

First try Example 61, a simple lick in the **key of E**.

61

Now try Example 62, a similar lick to Example 61, but the release bend is used.

62

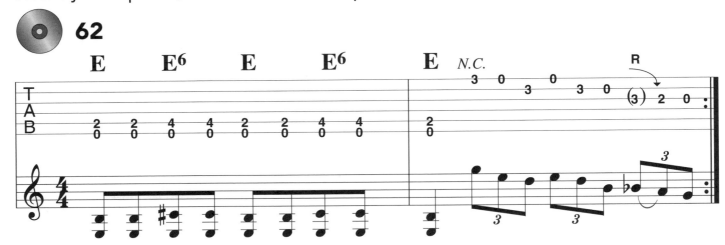

DOUBLE-NOTE LICKS

Throughout all the previous licks in this book only one note was played at a time. The **double-note lick** is the playing of two notes simultaneously, usually within a lead guitar pattern. The most common double-note licks are highlighted in the following diagrams.

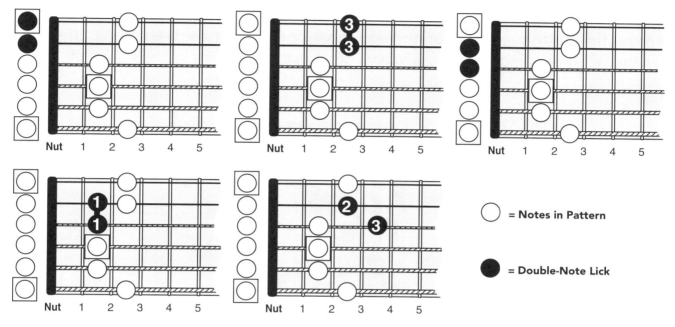

The double-note licks shown above are also highlighted in the following example. Listen carefully to the accompanying recording to hear the correct sound of these licks.

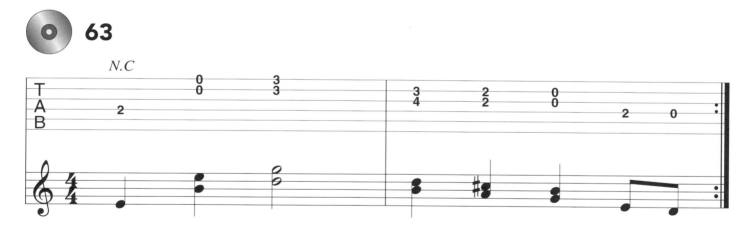

Try the following example which incorporates double-note licks and a standard E shuffle.

VIBRATO

This lesson introduces another popular lead guitar technique used frequently throughout a lick or solo, the **vibrato**. The vibrato is another technique controlled with the left hand finger which is fretting the note. This technique involves moving the string rapidly back and forth in the direction of the adjacent strings as the left hand finger is fretting the note.

In the following example vibrato is applied to the note on the **fifth** fret of the **2nd** string. Listen carefully to this example on the accompanying CD to hear the correct effect of this technique. Vibrato is indicated by a wavy line above the note.

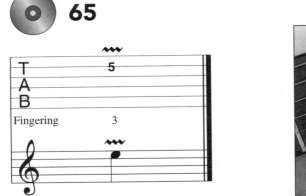

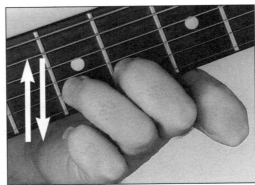

First try Example 66, a simple lick in the **key of E**.

Now try Example 67, the same lick as Example 66, but vibrato is used.

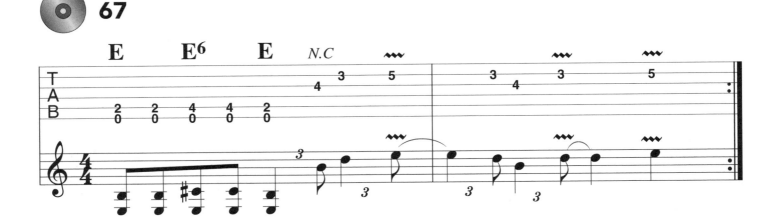

MORE TURNAROUND LICKS

Some variations of the turnaround lick are shown below.

TURNAROUND LICK NO. 2 IN E

68

TURNAROUND LICK NO. 1 IN A

The next two turnarounds are in the key of A

69

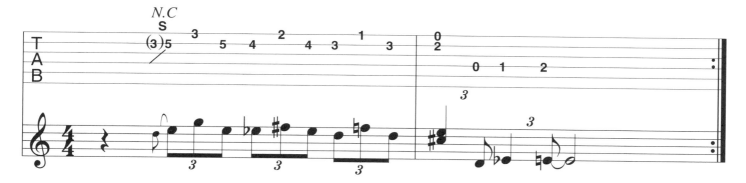

TURNAROUND LICK NO. 2 IN A

70

The following examples make use of all the techniques discussed so far.

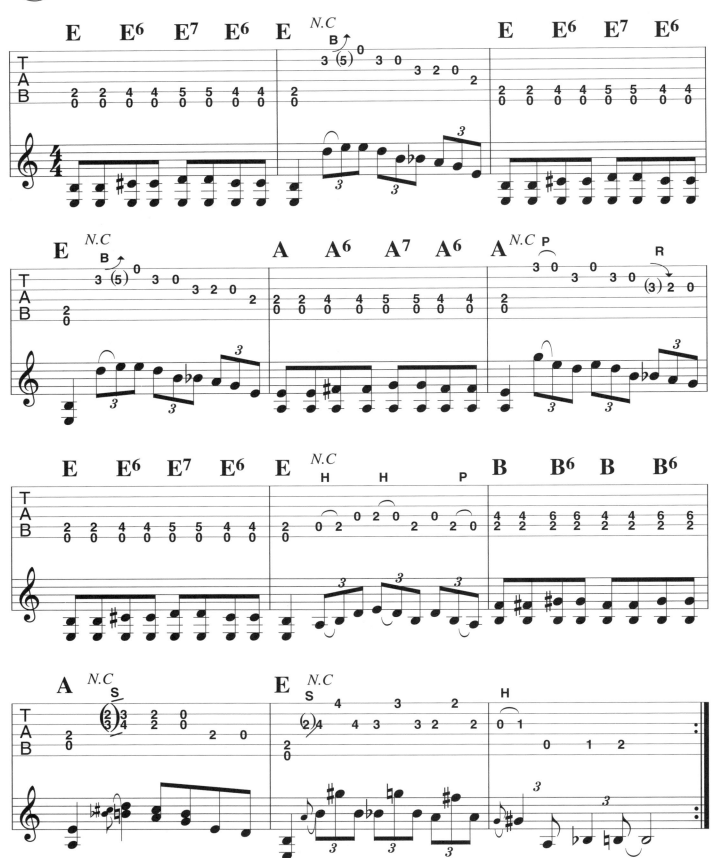

72

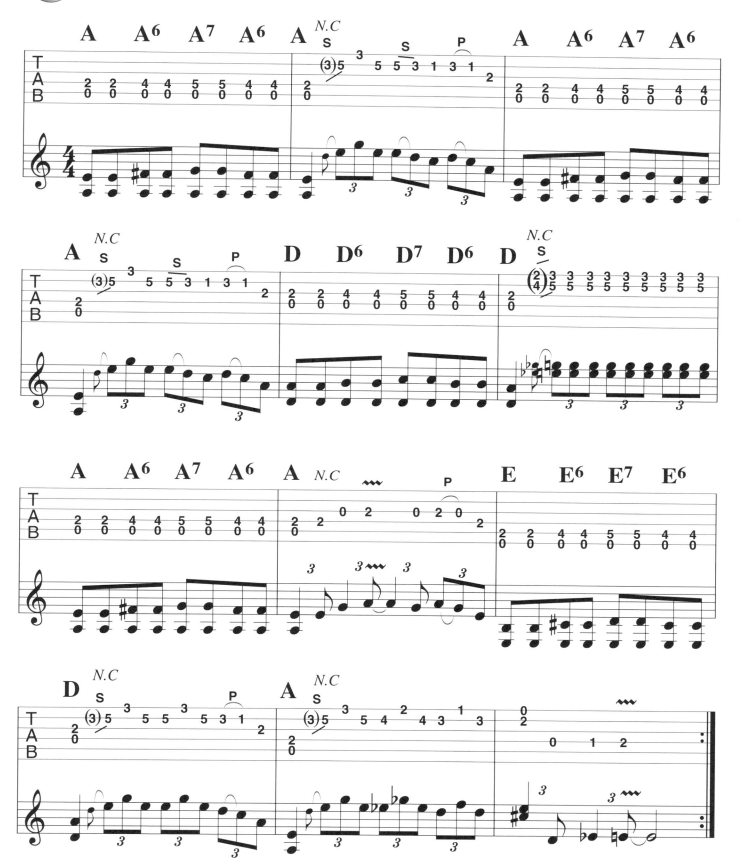

LESSON EIGHT

FINGERPICKING THE BLUES

This lesson introduces the use of fingerpicking in Blues. Before attempting the following lessons it would be helpful to have some previous experience of fingerpicking. *Progressive Fingerpicking Guitar* is recommended as an introductory manual to fingerpicking. Study the following points of fingerpicking basics.

RIGHT ARM POSITION

The correct position for your right arm is shown in the photograph below. Notice that your forearm rests on the **upper edge** of the guitar, just below the elbow. Be careful not to have your elbow hanging over the face of the guitar, or your right hand too far along the fretboard.

CORRECT   **INCORRECT**

RIGHT HAND POSITION

Study the photographs below for the correct hand position.

1. Rest the **forearm** on the upper edge of the guitar.
2. The **right hand** is at 90 degrees to the strings.
3. The **thumb** is parallel with the strings and clear of the other fingers.
4. **Pick** the strings over the Sound hole for the best sound.
5. **Do not** rest any part of your hand or fingers on the guitar body.

FRONT VIEW   **SIDE VIEW**

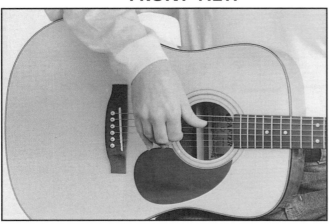

PICKING THE STRINGS

It is best to fingerpick the strings with your **fingernails** as this gives a better sound. You should let the fingernails of your right hand grow to a length that is comfortable for your playing e.g. 1/16" (1 millimetre) clear of the fingertip. The thumb nail should be longer. Fingernails should be shaped using a nail file (emery board) so that they have a rounded edge and flow smoothly off the string after it has been picked.

RIGHT HAND FINGER NAMES

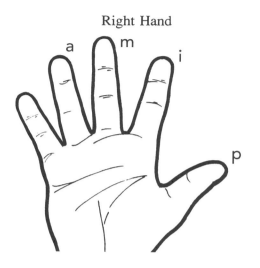

Right Hand

The right hand fingers are named using the following fingering symbols.

p = primary

i = index

m = middle

a = anular (ring finger)

The little finger is not used in fingerpicking.

PICKING WITH YOUR RIGHT HAND FINGERS

Start with your fingers not touching the strings, then pick the third string with your index finger (**i**) with an **upward** motion (do not pull the string outwards). Your finger should move from the first finger joint below the knuckle as shown in the diagram below. The sound is produced by the fingertip and the nail striking the string simultaneously. Move only your fingers, not your hand. The **i**, **m** and **a** fingers usually pick the **1st, 2nd** and **3rd** strings.

PICKING WITH YOUR THUMB

The **p** finger (**thumb**) usually picks the **6th, 5th** and **4th** strings. Pick with the lower side of your thumb as shown in the photograph below on the right. Pick with a **downward** motion and keep the thumb rigid, i.e. do not bend it like you do when picking with your fingers.

CONSTANT BASS LINE

A popular fingerpicking technique that features in Blues acoustic guitar is the constant bass line style. This technique involves the right hand thumb playing the root bass note of the chord repeatedly for the duration of the song. The easiest key to apply this style is the key of A because the root bass note of each chord in the key of A (A, D and E) can be played as an open string.

73

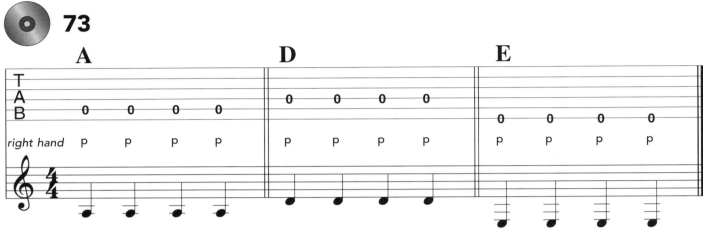

Now try applying the above constant bass lines to a 12 bar Blues progression in the key of A.

74

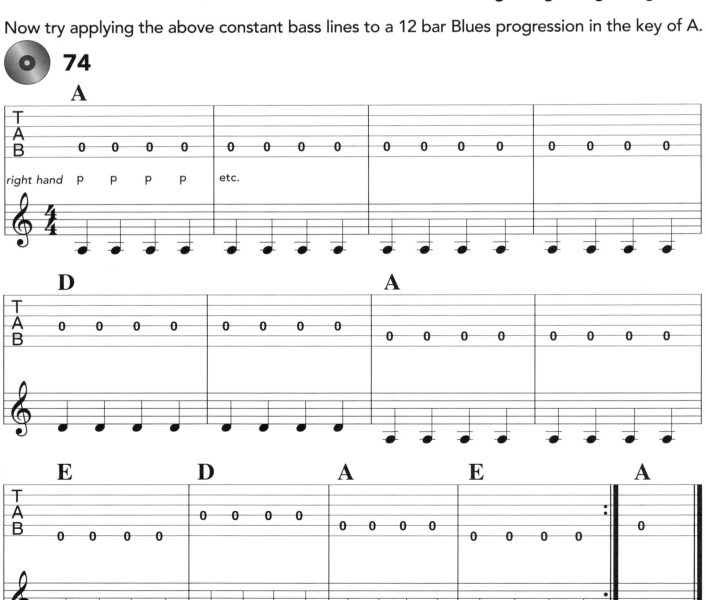

The constant bass line is used in conjuntion with notes from the A scales outlined earlier.

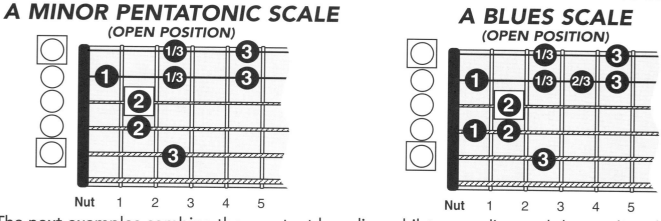

The next examples combine the constant bass line whilst ascending and descending the A scales shown above. The recommended fingering should only be used as a guide. Generally speaking the licks should be played with alternating 'm' and 'i' fingers. Feel free to vary this rule if you feel more comfortable breaking the alternating pattern on certain licks.

The next example combines a basic lick with the constant bass line.

78

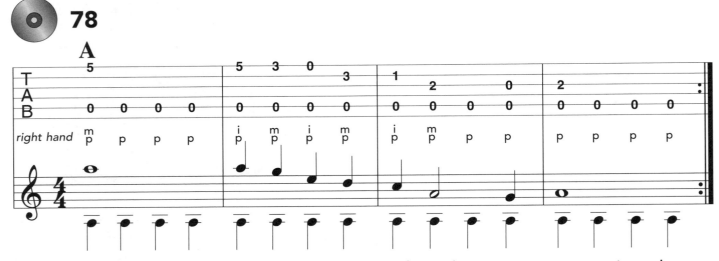

Now a 12 bar Blues progression using basic licks from the A minor pentatonic scale.

79

The next examples involve playing notes on the off beat, in between the bass notes.

 80

The following examples apply several lead guitar techniques studied in earlier lessons.

82

Now a complete 12 bar Blues progression using a variety of techniques.

CONSTANT BASS LINE IN THE KEY OF E

To use the constant bass line style in the key of E the following three bass lines are featured. This time it is necessary to finger the note B on the second fret of the fifth string for the duration of the B chord.

87

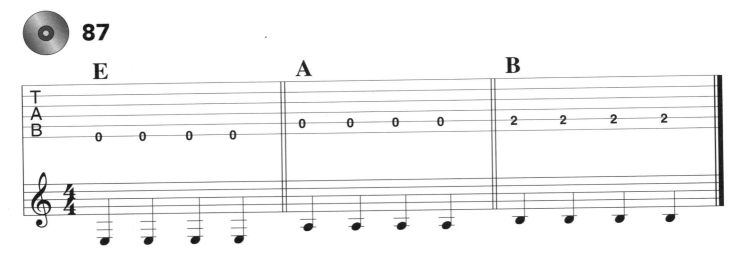

The E constant bass lines are used in conjunction with notes from the extended positions of the E scales studied earlier.

E MINOR PENTATONIC SCALE
(EXTENDED POSITION)

E BLUES SCALE
(EXTENDED POSITION)

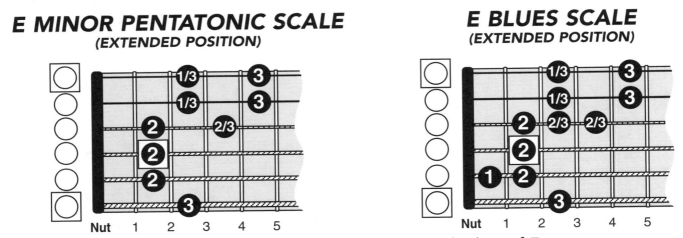

The next two exercises are constant bass line pieces in the key of E.

88

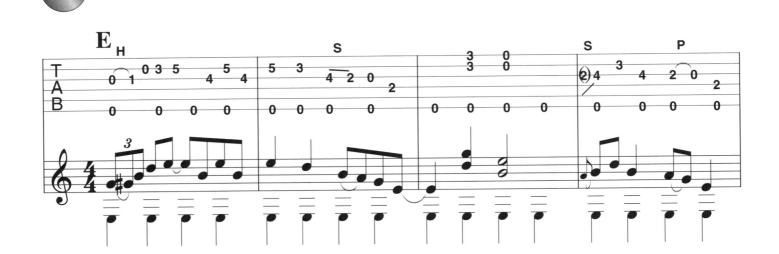

LESSON NINE

ALTERNATING THUMB STYLE

The other popular fingerpicking technique used in Blues is the **alternating thumb style**. For this style the thumb alternates between two bass notes on each beat of the bar, usually beginning with the root bass note of the current chord. The three alternating bass lines shown below are for the E, A and B7 chords; i.e. the three principal chords in the key of E.

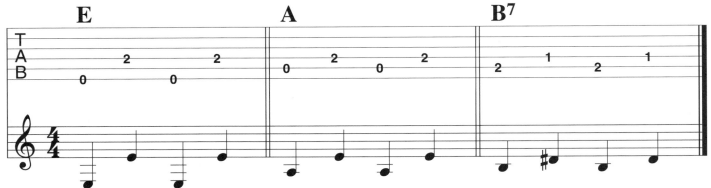

The following exercise combines the alternating thumb stlye with notes based around the E scales that have featured in earlier lessons. When using this style it is common practise to use an alternative fingering for the E major chord. Study accompanying diagram.

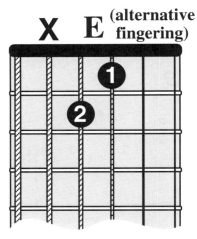

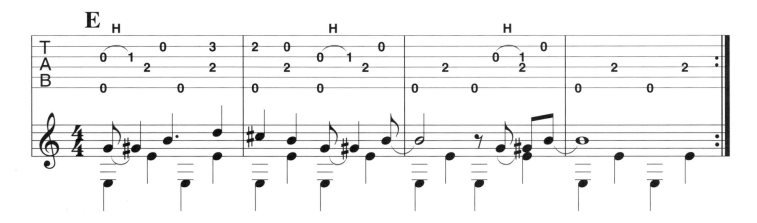

The next two exercises are based upon the A and B7 chords.

92

93

The following 8 bar Blues features the alternating thumb style.

94

The final example in this lesson is a Blues fingerpicking solo that contains a variety of techniques outlined throughout this book. An alternating thumb style is the basis of this piece but in bars 3, 8 and 9 the bass line changes to a 'walking' bass line. All of the chord shapes that are used are highlighted in the following diagrams. To simplify the music each chord shape is given a number rather than a name.

CHORD SHAPES USED IN EX. 95

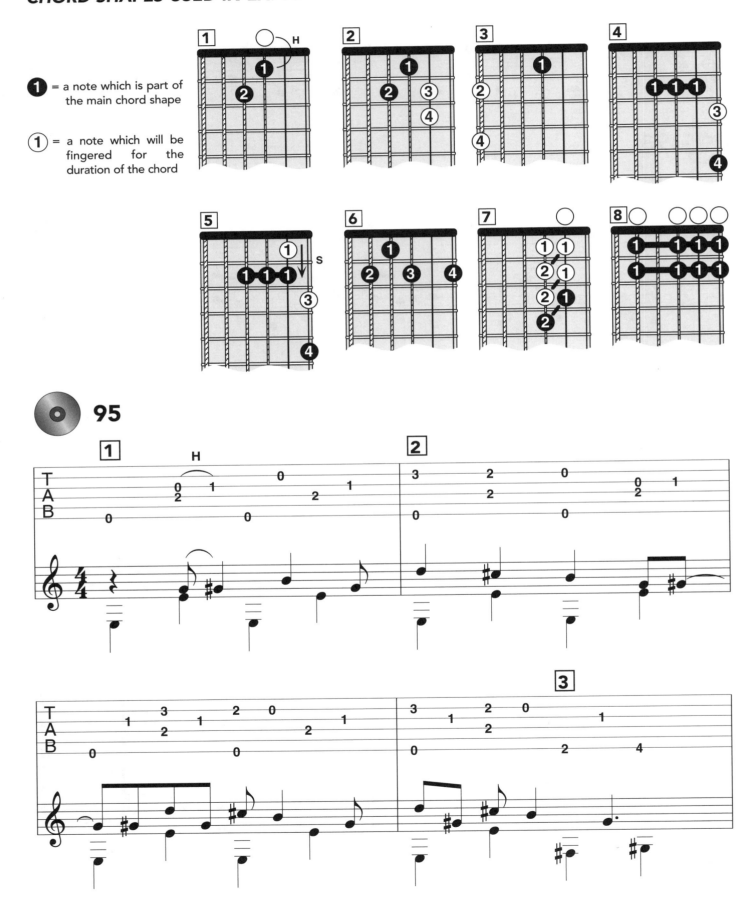

LESSON TEN

ACOUSTIC SLIDE GUITAR

Another popular style used in Blues involves using a **slide**, a metal or glass tube usually placed on the little finger of the left hand. This book only introduces the slide guitar style, for a more detailed description of this style see *Progressive Slide Guitar Technique* and *Progressive Slide Guitar Licks*. The slide is moved up or down the fretboard in the direction of the strings after a string is played. The slide does not fret the string, it only rests against the string.

The most important part of slide guitar technique is the use of the left hand. It will be necessary to practise some new basic fundamentals of left hand technique.

THE THUMB

The left hand thumb should be positioned behind the neck. Keep the thumb behind the second finger of the left hand and the face of the thumb against the back of the neck. The thumb must be kept straight.

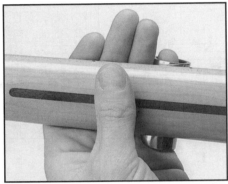 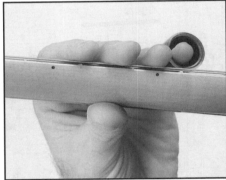

Thumb must be kept straight. *Keep the thumb behind the second finger.*

THE SLIDE

The slide is mostly used on the fourth finger of the left hand. It is rare a slide player would use another finger. It is important to keep the slide perfectly parallel to the fretwires.

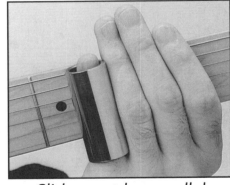

Slide must be parallel with fretwires.

DAMPING

With the slide on the fourth finger, at least one of the other fingers must lay across the strings behind the slide. This will help dampen the strings when the slide is lifted off the strings. It will also deaden any overtones which may occur when the slide is at certain frets.

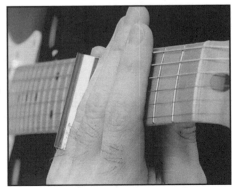

Damping with left hand fingers.

FRETTING

When a note is played with the slide it is necessary to hold the slide on the string directly above the fretwire and not before the fret wire (where a normal fretted note is held). The amount of pressure on the string will be something you will slowly get used to. When you move the slide try to keep the pressure as even as possible.

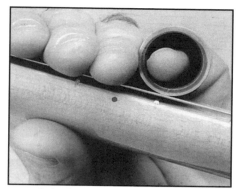

Hold slide above fret wire.

SLIDING

As you slide from one fret to another, it is important to keep the slide parallel to the frets. The thumb must trail behind the neck with the left hand fingers still damping the strings. The shape of the left hand should not alter as you move up and down the fretboard.

SLIDE SCALE PATTERNS

The most common slide scale patterns are shown below in the Key of E.

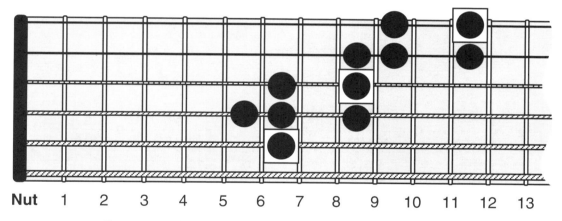

SLIDE SCALE PATTERN - KEY OF E

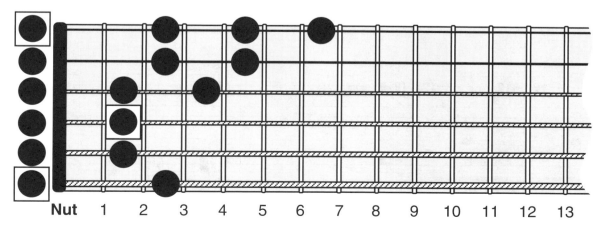

SLIDE SCALE PATTERN - KEY OF E (OPEN POSITION)

The following slide examples are played within the slide scales shown on the previous page.

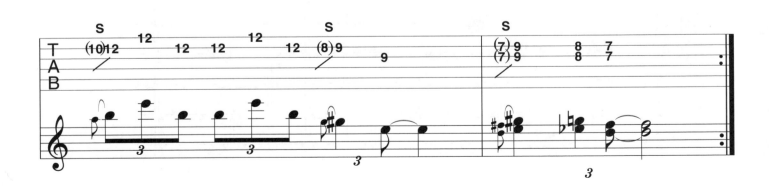

The following example combines a shuffle rhythm and some basic slide licks. Note: it is ok to play the turnaround lick in the final 2 bars as normal fretted notes with your fingers rather than play the notes as a slide lick.

98

The following slide example utilises the constant bass line.

 99

APPENDICES

THE RUDIMENTS OF MUSIC

The musical alphabet consists of 7 letters: **A B C D E F G**

Music is written on a **STAFF**, which consists of 5 parallel lines between which there are 4 spaces.

MUSIC STAFF

THE TREBLE OR 'G' CLEF is placed at the beginning of each staff line.

TREBLE or 'G' CLEF ⟶

This clef indicates the position of the note G. (It is an old fashioned method of writing the letter G, with the centre of the clef being written on the second staff line.)

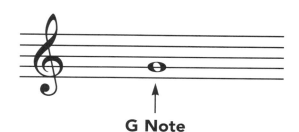

G Note

The other lines and spaces on the staff are named as such:

Extra notes can be added by the use of short lines, called **LEGER LINES**.

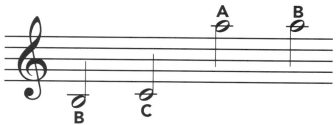

When a note is placed on the staff its head indicates its position, e.g.:

This is a G NOTE   **This is a C NOTE**

When the note head is below the middle staff line the stem points upward and when the head is above the middle line the stem points downward. A note placed on the middle line (**B**) can have its stem pointing either up or down.

BAR LINES are drawn across the staff, which divides the music into sections called **BARS** or **MEASURES**. A **DOUBLE BAR LINE** signifies either the end of the music, or the end of an important section of it.

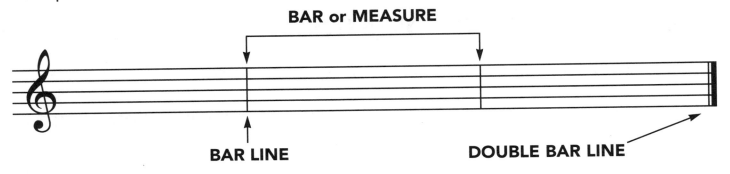

NOTE VALUES

The table below sets out the most common notes used in music and their respective time values (i.e. length of time held). For each note value there is an equivalent rest, which indicates a period of silence.

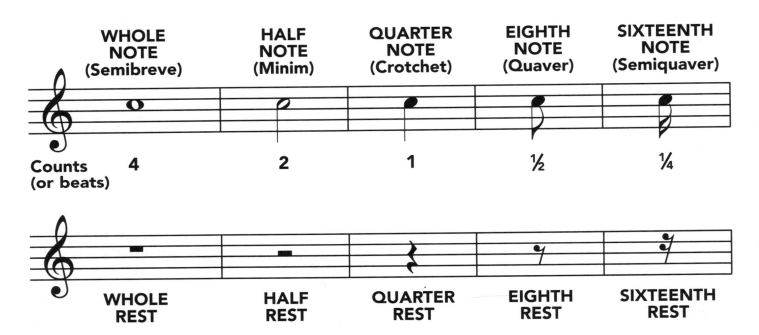

If a **DOT** is placed after a note it increases the value of that note by half, e.g.

DOTTED HALF NOTE	𝅗𝅥•	(2 + 1) = 3 counts
DOTTED QUARTER NOTE	♩•	(1 + ½) = 1½ counts
DOTTED WHOLE NOTE	𝅝•	(4 + 2) = 6 counts

A **TIE** is a curved line joining two or more notes of the same pitch, where the second note(s) **IS NOT PLAYED** but its time value is added tot hat of the first note. Here are two examples:

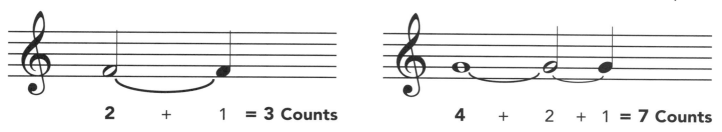

In both of these examples only the first note is played.

TIME SIGNATURES

At the beginning of each piece of music, after the treble clef, is the **TIME SIGNATURE**.

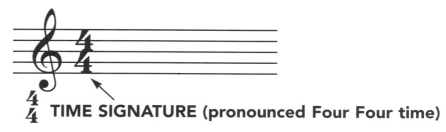

The time signature indicates the number of beats per bar (the top number) and the type of note receiving one beat (the bottom number). For example:

4 – this indicates 4 beats per bar.

4 – this indicates that each beat is worth a quarter note (crotchet).

Thus in $\frac{4}{4}$ time there must be the equivalent of 4 quarter note beats per bar, e.g.

$\frac{4}{4}$ is the most common time signature and is sometimes represented by this symbol called **COMMON TIME**.

COMMON TIME

The other time signature used in this book is Three Four Time written $\frac{3}{4}$.

$\frac{3}{4}$ indicates 3 quarter note beats per bar, e.g.

SCALES

A scale can be defined as a series of notes, in alphabetical order, going from any given note to its octave and based upon some form of set pattern. The pattern upon which most scales are based involves a set sequence of **tones** and/or **semitones**. On the guitar, a tone is two frets and a semitone is one fret. As an example, the **B** note is a tone higher than **A**, (two frets), whereas the **C** note is only a semitone higher than **B** (one fret). Of the other natural notes in music, **E** and **F** are a semitone apart, and all the others are a tone apart.

NATURAL NOTES

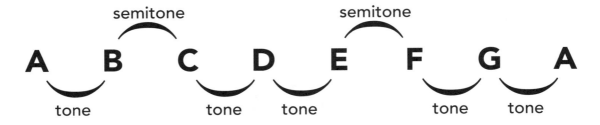

In music theory, a tone may be referred to as a **step** and a semitone as a **half-step**.

The main types of scales that you need to become familiar with are the **chromatic**, **major**, **minor**, **minor pentatonic** and **blues** scales.

THE CHROMATIC SCALE

The **chromatic** scale is based upon a sequence of **semitones** only and this includes every possible note within one octave. Here is the **C chromatic scale**.

C   C♯   D   D♯   E   F   F♯   G   G♯   A   A♯   B   C

The same scale could be written out using flats, however it is more common to do this when descending, as such;

C   B   B♭   A   A♭   G   G♭   F   E   E♭   D   D♭   C

Because each chromatic scale contains every possible note within one octave, once you have learnt one you have basically learnt them all. As an example, the **A** chromatic scale (written below) contains exactly the same notes as the **C** chromatic scale, the only difference between them being the note upon which they commence. This starting note, in all scales, is referred to as the **tonic** or **key note**.

THE A CHROMATIC SCALE

A   A♯   B   C   C♯   D   D♯   E   F   F♯   G   G♯   A

THE MAJOR SCALE

The most common scale in Western music is called the **major scale**. This scale is based upon a sequence of both tones and semitones, and is sometimes referred to as a **diatonic** scale. Here is the major scale sequence;

TONE	TONE	SEMITONE	TONE	TONE	TONE	SEMITONE
T	T	S	T	T	T	S

Starting on the **C** note and following through this sequence gives the **C major** scale;

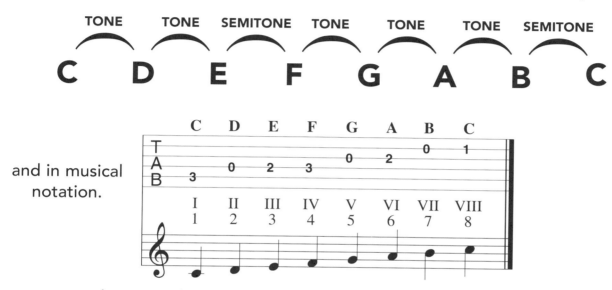

and in musical notation.

Roman numerals are used to number each note of the major scale. Thus **F** is the **fourth** note of the **C major** scale, **G** is the **fifth**, and so on.

The major scale will always give the familiar sound of **DO, RE, MI, FA, SO, LA, TI, DO**.

The major scale **always** uses the same sequence of tones and semitones, no matter what note is used as the tonic. The table below list the 13 most commonly used major scales.

You will notice that, in order to maintain the correct sequence of tones and semitones, all major scales except **C major** involve the use of either sharps or flats. You will notice, when playing these scales, that they all maintain the familiar sound of **DO, RE, MI, FA SO, LA, TI, DO**.

	T	T	S	T	T	T	S
C MAJOR	C	D	E	F	G	A	B	C
G MAJOR	G	A	B	C	D	E	F♯	G
D MAJOR	D	E	F♯	G	A	B	C♯	D
A MAJOR	A	B	C♯	D	E	F♯	G♯	A
E MAJOR	E	F♯	G♯	A	B	C♯	D♯	E
B MAJOR	B	C♯	D♯	E	F♯	G♯	A♯	B
F♯ MAJOR	F♯	G♯	A♯	B	C♯	D♯	E♯	F♯
F MAJOR	F	G	A	B♭	C	D	E	F
B♭ MAJOR	B♭	C	D	E♭	F	G	A	B♭
E♭ MAJOR	E♭	F	G	A♭	B♭	C	D	E♭
A♭ MAJOR	A♭	B♭	C	D♭	E♭	F	G	A♭
D♭ MAJOR	D♭	E♭	F	G♭	A♭	B♭	C	D♭
G♭ MAJOR	G♭	A♭	B♭	C♭	D♭	E♭	F	G♭
Roman Numerals	I	II	III	IV	V	VI	VII	VIII

THE MINOR SCALE

In western music there are three different minor scales. These are the **pure minor**, the **harmonic minor** and the **melodic minor**. Each features a slightly different sequence of tones and semitones, as illustrated in the examples below using **A** as the tonic.

A Minor 'Pure' Scale

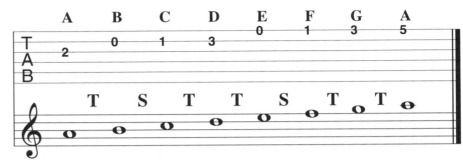

A Minor Harmonic – 7th note sharpened (called the LEADING NOTE):

A Minor Melodic – 6th and 7th notes sharpened when ascending and returned to natural when descending.

Of these three minor scales outlined above, the **melodic minor** is the most commonly used. The table below lists the 13 most commonly used minor scales.

	T	S	T	T	T	T	S	T	T	S	T	T	S	T	
A MELODIC MINOR	A	B	C	D	E	F#	G#	A	G♮	F♮	E	D	C	B	A
E MELODIC MINOR	E	F#	G	A	B	C#	D#	E	D♮	C♮	B	A	G	F#	E
B MELODIC MINOR	B	C#	D	E	F#	G#	A#	B	A♮	G♮	F#	E	D	C#	B
F# MELODIC MINOR	F#	G#	A	B	C#	D#	E#	F#	E♮	D♮	C#	B	A	G#	F#
C# MELODIC MINOR	C#	D#	E	F#	G#	A#	B#	C#	B♮	A♮	G#	F#	E	D#	C#
G# MELODIC MINOR	G#	A#	B	C#	D#	E#	G	G#	F#	E♮	D#	C#	B	A#	G#
D# MELODIC MINOR	D#	E#	F#	G#	A#	B#	D	D#	C#	B♮	A#	G#	F#	E#	D#
D MELODIC MINOR	D	E	F	G	A	B♮	C#	D	C♮	B♭	A	G	F	E	D
G MELODIC MINOR	G	A	B♭	C	D	E♮	F#	G	F♮	E♭	D	C	B♭	A	G
C MELODIC MINOR	C	D	E♭	F	G	A♮	B♮	C	B♭	A♭	G	F	E♭	D	C
F MELODIC MINOR	F	G	A♭	B♭	C	D♮	E♮	F	E♭	D♭	C	B♭	A♭	G	F
B♭ MELODIC MINOR	B♭	C	D♭	E♭	F	G♮	A♮	B♭	A♭	G♭	F	E♭	D♭	C	B♭
E♭ MELODIC MINOR	E♭	F	G♭	A♭	B♭	C♮	D♮	E♭	D♭	C♭	B♭	A♭	G♭	F♭	E♭

THE MINOR PENATONIC SCALE

The Minor Pentatonic Scale is constructed by taking the **1-♭3-4-5** and **♭7** notes from the major scale.

C major Scale

C Minor Pentatonic Scale

The most commonly used Minor Pentatonic Scales are outlined below.

C MINOR PENTATONIC	C	E♭	F	G	B♭	C
G MINOR PENTATONIC	G	B♭	C	D	F	G
D MINOR PENTATONIC	D	F	G	A	C	D
A MINOR PENTATONIC	A	C	D	E	G	A
E MINOR PENTATONIC	E	G	A	B	D	E
B MINOR PENTATONIC	B	D	E	F#	A	B
F# MINOR PENTATONIC	F#	A	B	C#	E	F#
F MINOR PENTATONIC	F	A♭	B♭	C	E♭	F
B♭ MINOR PENTATONIC	B♭	D♭	E♭	F	A♭	B♭
E♭ MINOR PENTATONIC	E♭	G♭	A♭	B♭	D♭	E♭
A♭ MINOR PENTATONIC	A♭	C♭	D♭	E♭	G♭	A♭
D♭ MINOR PENTATONIC	D♭	F♭	G♭	A♭	C♭	D♭
G♭ MINOR PENTATONIC	G♭	A	C♭	D♭	F♭	G♭

THE BLUES SCALE

The Blues Scale is the same as the Minor Pentatonic Scale except the ♭**5** note of the major scale is also used.

C Minor Pentatonic Scale

C Blues Scale

The most commonly used Blues Scales are shown below.

C BLUES SCALE	C	E♭	F	G♭	G	B♭	C
G BLUES SCALE	G	B♭	C	D♭	D	F	G
D BLUES SCALE	D	F	G	A♭	A	C	D
A BLUES SCALE	A	C	D	E♭	E	G	A
E BLUES SCALE	E	G	A	B♭	B	D	E
B BLUES SCALE	B	D	E	F	F#	A	B
F# BLUES SCALE	F#	A	B	C	C#	E	F#
F BLUES SCALE	F	A♭	B♭	B	C	E♭	F
B♭ BLUES SCALE	B♭	D♭	E♭	E	F	A♭	B♭
E♭ BLUES SCALE	E♭	G♭	A♭	A	B♭	D♭	E♭
A♭ BLUES SCALE	A♭	C♭	D♭	D	E♭	G♭	A♭
D♭ BLUES SCALE	D♭	F♭	G♭	G	A♭	C♭	D♭
G♭ BLUES SCALE	G♭	A	C♭	C	D♭	F♭	G♭

KEYS AND KEY SIGNATURES

When music is talked of as being in a particular key, it means that the melody is based upon notes of the major scale (or minor scale) with the same name e.g. in the **key of C, C major** scale notes (i.e. **C, D, E, F, G, A** and **B**) will occur more frequently than notes that do not belong to the **C** scale (i.e. sharpened and flattened notes).

In the **key of G, G** scale notes will be most common (i.e. the notes **G, A, B, C, D, E** and **F♯** will occur frequently). You will notice here that **F♯** occurs rather than F natural. However, rather than add a sharp to every **F** note, an easier method is used whereby a sharp sign is placed on the **F** line (the top one) of the staff at the beginning of each line. This is referred to as the **key signature**: thus the key signature of **G major** is **F♯**.

Written below are the key signatures for all major scales so far discussed.

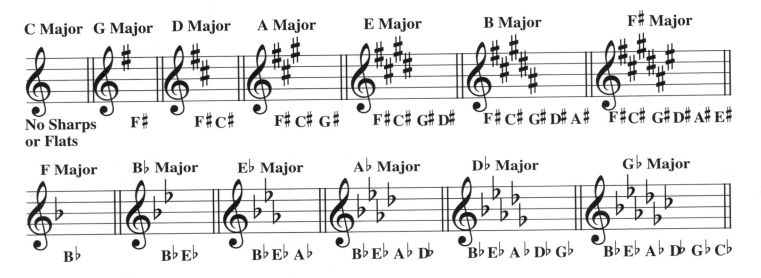

It can be seen, then, that each key signature is a shorthand representation of the scale, showing only the sharps or flats which occur in that scale. Where an additional sharp or flat occurs, it is not included as part of the key signature, but is written in the music, e.g. in the **key of G**, if a **D♯** note occurs, the sharp sign will be written immediately before the **D** note, **not** at the beginning of the line as part of the key signature.

RELATIVE KEYS

if you compare the **A minor** "pure" minor scale with the **C major** scale you will notice that they contain the same notes (except starting on a different note). Because of this, these two scales are referred to as "relatives"; **A minor** is the relative minor of **C major** and vice versa.

Major Scale: C Major

Relative Minor Scale: A Minor (pure)

The harmonic and melodic minor scale variations are also relatives of the same major scale, e.g. **A harmonic** and **A melodic minor** are relatives of **C major**.

For every major scale (and ever major chord) there is a relative minor scale which is based upon the **6th note** of the major scale. This is outlined in the table below.

MAJOR KEY (I)	C	D♭	D	E♭	E	F	F♯	G♭	G	A♭	A	B♭	B
RELATIVE MINOR KEY (VI)	Am	B♭m	Bm	Cm	C♯m	Dm	D♯m	E♭m	Em	Fm	F♯m	Gm	G♯m

Both the major and the relative minor share the same key signature, as illustrated in the examples below:

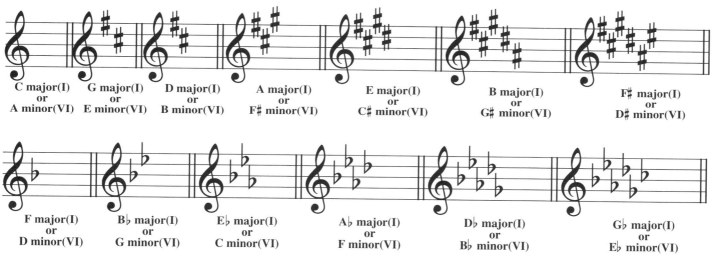

The sharpened **7th** note that occurs in the relative minor key is never included as part of the key signature. Because each major and relative minor share the same key signature, you will need to know how to distinguish between the two keys. For example, if given a piece with the key signature of **F♯** thus:

It could indicate either the **key of G major** or its relative, **E minor**. The most accurate way of determining the key is to look through the melody for the sharpened **7th** note of the **E minor** scale (**D♯**). The presence of this note will indicate the minor key. If the **7th** note is present, but not sharpened, then the key is more likely to be the relative major (i.e. **D** natural notes would suggest the **key of G major**).

Another method is to look at the first and last chords of the progression. These chords usually (but not always) indicate the key of the piece. If the piece starts and/or finishes with **Em** chords then the key is more likely to be **E minor**.

OTHER BLUES BOOKS IN THE PROGRESSIVE SERIES

PROGRESSIVE BLUES LEAD GUITAR METHOD
FOR BEGINNER TO ADVANCED

This book takes a unique approach to learning Blues lead guitar. The most common scale used in Blues – the minor pentatonic scale, is used immediately to make music. The scale is learned in five basic positions which cover the whole fretboard, along with a variety of licks and solos demonstrating all the important techniques such as slides, vibrato and note bending, as used by all the great Blues players.

PROGRESSIVE BLUES LEAD GUITAR TECHNIQUE
INTERMEDIATE TO ADVANCED

The central approach of this book is the development of musical technique, dealing with rhythm as it applies to lead guitar playing and concentrating on the development of phrasing and timing and how to really get the most out of the notes you play. Along the way, the book introduces the Blues scale and other important scales and arpeggios commonly used by Blues players. Also contains lots of great solos.

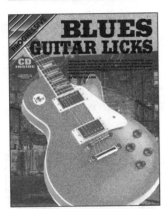

PROGRESSIVE BLUES GUITAR LICKS
FOR BEGINNER TO ADVANCED

Packed full of Blues guitar licks and solos incorporating styles and techniques used by the world's greatest Blues players. Includes sections on turnarounds, intro's and endings, call and response, dynamics and learning from other instruments. The licks cover a variety of styles such as shuffles, traditional slow Blues, Boogie, Jazz style Blues and R&B and Funk grooves. Also includes examples demonstrating how different licks can be put together to form whole solos, opening up endless possibilities for improvisation.

PROGRESSIVE BLUES GUITAR SOLOS
INTERMEDIATE TO ADVANCED

Contains a great selection of Blues solos in a variety of styles reflecting the whole history of the Blues tradition from early Delta Blues to contemporary Blues Rock. Demonstrates various methods of creating solos along with sections on vocal style phrasing, call and response, developing a theme, dynamics and the use of space. Many of the solos are written in the styles of Blues legends like Muddy Waters, John Lee Hooker, BB, Albert and Freddy King, Buddy Guy, Albert Collins, Peter Green, Magic Sam, Otis Rush, Eric Clapton and Stevie Ray Vaughan.

PROGRESSIVE BLUES RHYTHM GUITAR METHOD
FOR BEGINNING BLUES GUITARISTS

A comprehensive introduction to the world of Blues rhythm guitar playing. Uses a variety of left and right hand techniques to help the student gain control of timing and rhythms which are essential to creating good Blues rhythm parts. The book contains a study of both open and moveable chord shapes, before moving on to single and double note riffs which include many of the classic Blues sounds.